D1263573

Super Structures
Charles Kuonen Suspension Bridge

Dash!
LEVELED READERS
An Imprint of Abdo Zoom • abdopublishing.com

3

3 Dash!
LEVELED READERS

Level 1 – Beginning
Short and simple sentences with familiar words or patterns for children who are beginning to understand how letters and sounds go together.

Level 2 – Emerging
Longer words and sentences with more complex language patterns for readers who are practicing common words and letter sounds.

Level 3 – Transitional
More developed language and vocabulary for readers who are becoming more independent.

abdopublishing.com

Published by Abdo Zoom, a division of ABDO, PO Box 398166, Minneapolis, Minnesota 55439.
Copyright © 2019 by Abdo Consulting Group, Inc. International copyrights reserved in all countries.
No part of this book may be reproduced in any form without written permission from the publisher.
Dash!™ is a trademark and logo of Abdo Zoom.

Printed in the United States of America, North Mankato, Minnesota.
052018
092018

Photo Credits: Alamy, iStock, Shutterstock
Production Contributors: Kenny Abdo, Jennie Forsberg, Grace Hansen, John Hansen
Design Contributors: Dorothy Toth, Neil Klinepier

Library of Congress Control Number: 2017960593

Publisher's Cataloging in Publication Data

Names: Murray, Julie, author.
Title: Charles Kuonen Suspension Bridge / by Julie Murray.
Description: Minneapolis, Minnesota : Abdo Zoom, 2019. | Series: Super structures |
    Includes online resources and index.
Identifiers: ISBN 9781532123108 (lib.bdg.) | ISBN 9781532124082 (ebook) |
    ISBN 9781532124570 (Read-to-me ebook)
Subjects: LCSH: Elevated pedestrian walkways--Juvenile literature. |
    Aerial walkways--Juvenile literature. | Architecture--building design--Juvenile literature. |
    Structural design--Juvenile literature.
Classification: DDC 624.2--dc23

Table of Contents

Charles Kuonen Suspension Bridge

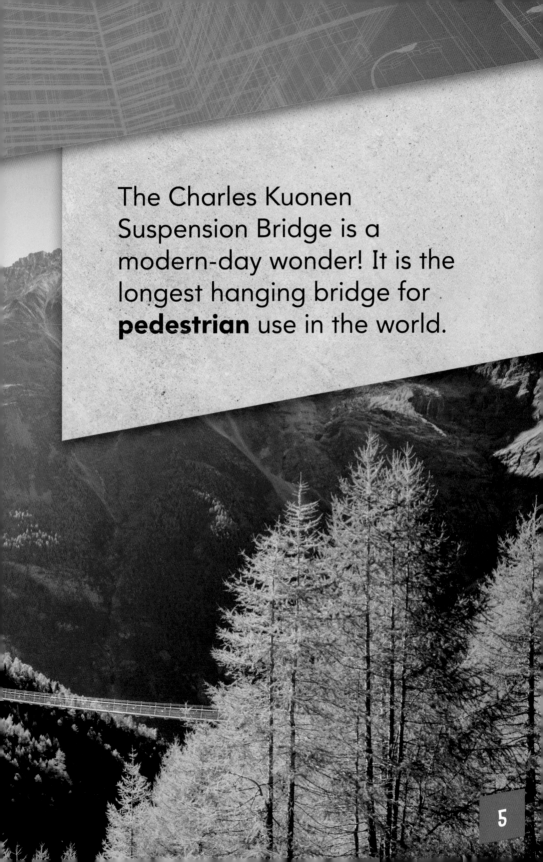

The Charles Kuonen Suspension Bridge is a modern-day wonder! It is the longest hanging bridge for **pedestrian** use in the world.

It is located in Randa, Switzerland. The bridge hangs over a large **ravine**.

The Bridge

The Swiss firm Swissrope constructed the record-breaking bridge. It cost more than $775,000 and only took 10 weeks to build! It opened in July 2017.

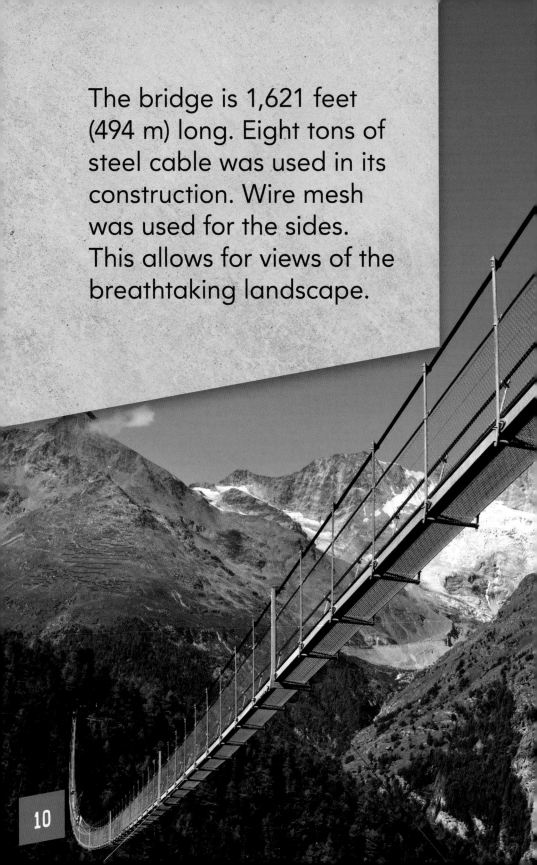

The bridge is 1,621 feet (494 m) long. Eight tons of steel cable was used in its construction. Wire mesh was used for the sides. This allows for views of the breathtaking landscape.

The path on the bridge is just over two feet (.6 m) wide. It is **single-file** walking both ways. The walkway is grated, so you can see straight down.

The bridge is 279 feet (85 m) off the ground at the highest point. It sways a bit. It is not recommended for those who are afraid of heights!

The Hike

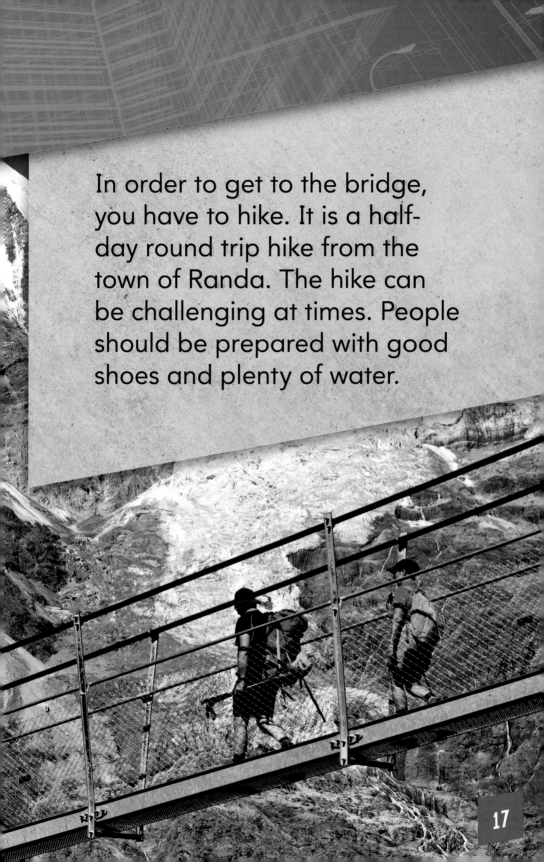

In order to get to the bridge, you have to hike. It is a half-day round trip hike from the town of Randa. The hike can be challenging at times. People should be prepared with good shoes and plenty of water.

The hike takes travelers through **Larchwood** forests. It also passes a viewing point, which stands at about 5,700 feet (1,737 m).

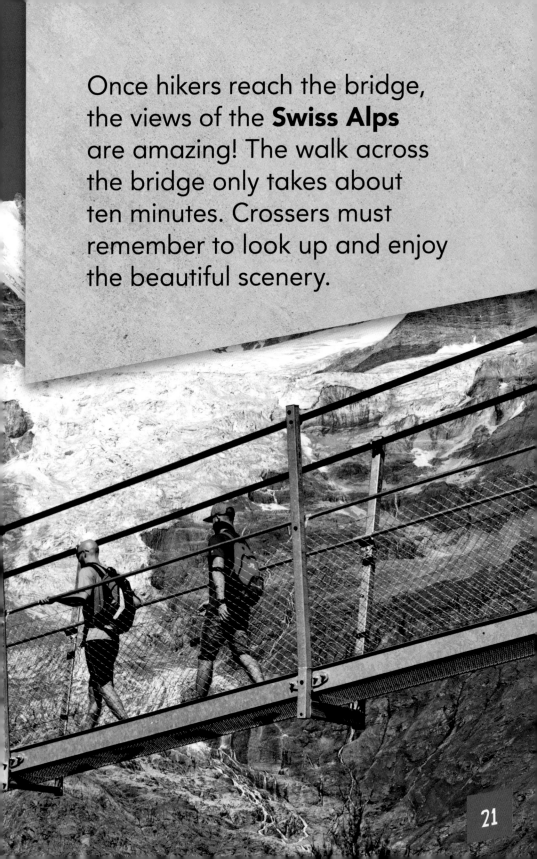

Once hikers reach the bridge, the views of the **Swiss Alps** are amazing! The walk across the bridge only takes about ten minutes. Crossers must remember to look up and enjoy the beautiful scenery.

More Facts

- The bridge is named after Charles Kuonen. He is a Swiss psychologist and is the primary sponsor of the bridge.

- The bridge shortens the Europaweg foot trail. It cuts off about four hours from this two-day hike in the Alps.

- The bridge is open from April to November. Because of the steel construction, hikers should avoid the bridge during lightning storms.

Glossary

Larch – a large, deciduous tree with short needles and cones.

pedestrian – a person who is walking.

ravine – a deep, narrow valley.

single-file – one behind another.

Swiss Alps – The Alpine region of Switzerland. The Alps are one of the highest and largest mountain ranges in the world.

Index

Online Resources

Booklinks
NONFICTION NETWORK
FREE! ONLINE NONFICTION RESOURCES

To learn more about Charles Kuonen Suspension Bridge, please visit **abdobooklinks.com**. These links are routinely monitored and updated to provide the most current information available.